Russia's Contribution to China's Surface Warfare Capabilities

Feeding the Dragon

AUTHOR

Paul Schwartz

A Report of the CSIS Russia and Eurasia Program

August 2015

CSIS | CENTER FOR STRATEGIC & INTERNATIONAL STUDIES

ROWMAN & LITTLEFIELD

Lanham • Boulder • New York • London

About CSIS

For over 50 years, the Center for Strategic and International Studies (CSIS) has worked to develop solutions to the world's greatest policy challenges. Today, CSIS scholars are providing strategic insights and bipartisan policy solutions to help decisionmakers chart a course toward a better world.

CSIS is a nonprofit organization headquartered in Washington, D.C. The Center's 220 full-time staff and large network of affiliated scholars conduct research and analysis and develop policy initiatives that look into the future and anticipate change.

Founded at the height of the Cold War by David M. Abshire and Admiral Arleigh Burke, CSIS was dedicated to finding ways to sustain American prominence and prosperity as a force for good in the world. Since 1962, CSIS has become one of the world's preeminent international institutions focused on defense and security; regional stability; and transnational challenges ranging from energy and climate to global health and economic integration.

Former U.S. senator Sam Nunn has chaired the CSIS Board of Trustees since 1999. Former deputy secretary of defense John J. Hamre became the Center's president and chief executive officer in 2000.

CSIS does not take specific policy positions; accordingly, all views expressed herein should be understood to be solely those of the author(s).

ISBN: 978-1-4422-5878-5 (pb); 978-1-4422-5879-2 (eBook)

Center for Strategic & International Studies
1616 Rhode Island Avenue, NW
Washington, DC 20036
202-887-0200 | www.csis.org

Rowman & Littlefield
4501 Forbes Boulevard
Lanham, MD 20706
301-459-3366 | www.rowman.com

Contents

Acknowledgments

This report is made possible by the generous support of the Carnegie Corporation of New York.

The author would like to thank all those who kindly agreed to review and comment on the report, including Dr. Carlo Kopp and Dr. Martin Andrew of Air Power Australia, Dr. Thomas Mahnken at the Johns Hopkins University School of Advanced International Studies, Zack Cooper of the Japan Chair at CSIS, and of course, Dr. Andrew Kuchins, Dr. Jeffrey Mankoff, and Oliver Backes with the Russia and Eurasia Program at CSIS. The report benefited greatly from their suggestions and comments.

1 | Introduction

China's rise to great power status is certain to be one of the most challenging geopolitical events of the twenty-first century. Since Deng Xiaoping initiated major economic reforms in 1978, China has made enormous headway in developing its national power. The driving force behind China's rise has been the rapid expansion of its economy, which has been growing at an average rate of nearly 8 percent per year since reforms were initiated, and appears poised to grow at reasonably high levels for the foreseeable future. China's sustained growth recently made it the second largest economy in the world, with a GDP of over $10 trillion.

More recently, China has also made great strides in translating its growing economic power into military power. China's officially announced defense budget for 2014 was approximately $132 billion, which represented an increase of 12.2 percent over the budget for the previous year. Moreover, since the official budget tends to understate actual spending, the true amount may have been up to 40 percent higher.[1] Already the second largest in the world, China's defense budget is likely to reach $145 billion in 2015.[2]

With increased spending has come rapid military modernization. Since China's most pressing territorial disputes remain centered on its maritime regions, modernization of China's navy has received especially high priority. China's navy (the People's Liberation Army Navy or PLAN) has received new ships, submarines, aircraft, and supporting systems at a rapid rate. Until recently, though, China's defense industry remained limited in its ability to produce advanced systems on its own, leading China to rely on foreign sources for advanced military equipment.

Russia has been China's principal source of foreign military technology since the Cold War. Since 1991, Russia has transferred over $30 billion of arms and military technology to China.[3] During the first years after the Soviet collapse, the arms trade between Beijing and Moscow ramped up gradually. But the pace quickened after the Third Taiwan Strait Crisis in 1996, which lent an increased sense of urgency to China's naval modernization efforts.

---

1. "China's Military Spending: At the Double," *Economist*, March 15, 2014.
2. Edward Wong and Chris Buckley, "China's Military Budget Increasing 10%," *New York Times*, March 4, 2015.
3. Stockholm International Peace Research Institute (SIPRI) Arms Transfer Database, http://www.sipri.org/databases/armstransfers; and Linda Jakobsen, Paul Holtom, Dean Knox, and Jingchao Peng, *China's Energy and Security Relations with Russia: Hopes, Frustrations and Uncertainties* (Stockholm: SIPRI, October 2011), 14.

Arms sales remained at a relatively high level for the next ten years, but declined sharply starting in 2006.

By then, China's indigenous defense industry had improved substantially, leaving Beijing somewhat less dependent on Russian arms imports. For its part, Russia had become increasingly concerned about China's reverse engineering activities, and increasingly reluctant to provide advanced weapons to a country many strategists still viewed as a potential future adversary. Recently Moscow and Beijing have been engaged in negotiations for a number of significant new transactions, indicating that Russian arms transfers may once again be on the increase.

Russian weapon systems and related technology have proven especially important for the development of China's naval surface warfare capabilities. Incorporation of Russian air defense technology, long-range sensors, and anti-ship cruise missile (ASCM) systems has enabled China's maritime forces to significantly improve both their defensive and offensive capabilities. By integrating advanced Russian air defense platforms with new Chinese air defense systems built using Russian technology, China's surface warships have become increasingly capable of fending off U.S. air strikes and long-range missile attacks. This development has made China's fleet much less dependent on land-based air defense systems, allowing it in turn to operate at increasingly greater distances from shore. In a similar vein, the deployment of highly capable Russian ASCM systems alongside a whole new generation of Chinese anti-ship missiles, many derived from Russian technology, has enhanced the ability of China's maritime forces to conduct long-range precision strikes against U.S. surface warships. The increased ability to threaten U.S. surface forces operating in the western Pacific is essential for giving effect to China's strategy of denying rival navies access to waters and airspace Beijing considers strategically vital.

General Scope

Russian arms and technology transfers have been and continue to be crucial for development of China's anti-access capability in the western Pacific. Despite a slowdown in military sales since 2006, Russia continues to transfer arms and technology to China on a fairly large scale to this day, and most of the items transferred are geared to supporting to China's anti-access programs. Moreover, Russia continues to provide technology assistance for indigenous Chinese weapon programs, while China continues to absorb the wide array of military technology previously transferred to it by Russia. These activities continue to pay dividends for China, which has been steadily producing a range of new weapon systems derived from Russian technology. While China has been increasingly manufacturing many of its own weapon systems domestically, real questions remain about the level of innovation in China's defense industry. Often what is described as "innovative" by the Chinese is actually a relatively incremental improvement on foreign (and in many cases Russian) technology.

While Russian technology has bolstered Chinese military capabilities in several areas, this report will be limited to an examination of Russia's contributions in just one area,

China's emerging surface and anti-surface naval warfare capabilities. Specifically, the report will focus on two issues: (1) how Russian arms transfers since the Cold War have affected China's ability to conduct surface and anti-surface warfare operations against U.S. warships operating in the western Pacific and (2) how such transfers have impacted China's ability to provide air defense for its surface fleet against air and precision missile strikes by the U.S. military.

Focusing the topic in this way sheds light on several important questions, some of which are currently the subject of intense debate. These include the following:

- What kinds of weapons and technology has Russia actually provided for China's surface warfare capabilities since the end of the Cold War?

- How have such weapons and technology contributed to the development of China's anti-access capabilities?

- Which of these capabilities are most problematic for the United States and its allies?

- How much have Chinese surface warfare systems and technology really caught up to Russia's?

- In which areas could China continue to benefit from Russian arms and technology transfers?

Although this report will attempt to answer these questions with regard to anti-surface warfare and naval air defense, those answers should also provide some insights into broader questions surrounding Sino-Russian arms and technology transfers in general. In this manner, the study should shed light on the impact of Russian arms and technology transfers on China's military as a whole.

Terms of Reference

For purposes of this report, defense assistance is defined broadly to include Russian transfers of completed platforms (e.g., entire navy ships), fully assembled weapon systems (e.g., air defense systems), and individual components. Defense assistance also includes technology transfer to the extent used by China to develop or enhance its indigenous weapon designs. This report also considers systems developed by China through reverse engineering of previously transferred Russian systems to be the product of Russian defense assistance. Including reverse engineered systems is appropriate for two reasons. First, it is often impossible to distinguish cases in which China has illicitly copied a Russian system from those in which China has acted with Russia's approval, as such matters are not always discussed publicly. More importantly, Russia's election to continue to assist China despite its reverse engineering efforts provides reasonably strong evidence of Russia's tacit acceptance of such activities.

Finally, a brief word about sources seems in order. This report relies exclusively on open source information. This report relies wherever possible on authoritative sources, including to the extent available official government publications and articles and reports prepared by recognized authorities in the field of Russian and Chinese naval technology. Such materials are not always available for every aspect of this report, however, in which case a variety of sources have been consulted. While every effort has been made to identify and use the most reliable sources, it should be acknowledged up front that there is often considerable disagreement among such sources, and they are not always of equal reliability. Sometimes sources disagree on even very basic points, such as whether Beijing has actually acquired a certain Russian system. Despite these limitations, it is quite possible to obtain an overall sense of Russia's contribution to China's surface warfare capabilities from open sources. Still, in evaluating the findings, such limitations should be kept in mind.

2 | Context

China's Anti-Access Strategy

During the latter years of the Cold War, China's military strategy remained focused on fighting and winning a major land war against the Soviet Union. This strategy called for China to mount an active defense along the Sino-Soviet border to blunt a projected large-scale Soviet offensive, and ultimately take the offensive itself when conditions warranted.[1] Fulfilling this strategy required China to maintain a mass army equipped with vast amounts of ground-based weapon systems, including tanks, artillery, rocket launchers, and other systems. Such a strategy also accorded reasonably well with China's military traditions, which had for centuries emphasized the continental mission of fending off foreign invasion. Given such a focus, the PLAN had always been relegated to a secondary role of supporting the army, by transporting men and materiel along the coast, and by protecting the army's flanks from seaborne attack. Until the mid-1980s, the People's Republic had never seriously contemplated expanding its maritime capabilities beyond what was required to fulfill this limited mission.

By the mid-1980s, however, China's leaders began to question the underlying premise of that strategy, namely, that a land-based war with the Soviets remained the most likely conflict scenario facing China. With the Soviet Union still locked in a titanic struggle with the West, it seemed increasingly unlikely that the Soviets would simultaneously undertake a large-scale war with China. As the Soviet threat receded, a variety of heretofore low-priority threats gained greater prominence. Such threats included especially the possibility of armed conflict arising on China's periphery over long-standing border disputes with its neighbors. Such a conflict might take many forms and could vary significantly in intensity, but was likely to remain limited in nature, being constrained in one way or another by the limited political objectives involved. Most importantly, such conflicts would not always take place on land. Instead, China would now have to focus equally on defending its maritime territories and interests in the nearby seas.[2]

Defending China's territorial interests against a range of potential adversaries both on land and at sea required an entire new strategy. Moreover, fighting the kinds of limited

---

1. Paul H. B. Godwin, "The PLA Faces the Twenty-First Century: Reflections on Technology, Doctrine, Strategy, and Operations," in *China's Military Faces the Future*, ed. James R. Lilley and David Shambaugh (Armonk, NY: M.E. Sharpe, 1999), 45.
2. Ibid., 48.

wars contemplated by the new strategy required new military capabilities as well. While the People's Liberation Army (PLA) was reasonably prepared to deal with potential land conflicts on its periphery, defending China's maritime interests against potential seaborne threats constituted a radically new mission. This mission gained even greater prominence following resolution of most of China's remaining border disputes in the years following the Cold War.[3] Consequently, for the first time in its history, the PLA found itself focused primarily on handling potential disputes in China's nearby maritime regions. To meet these changed circumstances, the Chinese military adopted a new "offshore defense" strategy in the mid-1980s. This new strategy was the brainchild of Admiral Liu Huaqing, one of the PLAN's most forward-thinking military commanders. Under this new strategy, the role of the army was to be diminished, while the navy's (and the air force's) was to be elevated significantly. No longer would the PLAN focus merely on providing coastal defense to support the army's land operations. Henceforth, it would take the lead in defending China's maritime interests in its nearby seas.[4]

The resulting offshore defense strategy calls for the establishment of a defensive perimeter in China's near seas out to a range of up to 200 nautical miles. This perimeter would encompass the Yellow Sea, the East China Sea, the Taiwan Strait, much of the South China Sea, and areas around the Spratly Islands as well. This area is often referred to as the region falling within the so-called First Island Chain. While the primary focus of China's offshore defense strategy is to defend this perimeter, the strategy also calls for having some ability to impede operations in areas outside it as well.

China's offshore defense strategy is basically a sea denial strategy. Its primary objective is to prevent a potential maritime adversary from gaining access to contested maritime regions located within the defended perimeter, which is why U.S. analysts often refer to it as an anti-access strategy. If successful, China's anti-access strategy will give its military the freedom to conduct military operations within the contested maritime region as needed to achieve its strategic objectives. For example, in a future conflict over Taiwan, China's military leaders would need to deploy forces capable of preventing U.S. carrier strike groups from intervening in the conflict. China could also use the anti-access approach to protect the Chinese mainland from potential offshore attack or even outright invasion from the sea, a frequently recurring problem in Chinese history.

China's leaders recognize, of course, that waging a successful anti-access campaign against a technologically superior foe like the United States would be no easy feat. They also recognize that the PLAN cannot hope to match the United States in a head-to-head military contest anytime soon. Therefore, China's anti-access strategy relies on use of asymmetric means to keep U.S. forces out of contested maritime regions. Under this

---

3. Michael McDevitt, "The PLA Navy's Antiaccess Role in a Taiwan Contingency," in *The Chinese Navy: Expanding Capabilities, Evolving Roles*, ed. Phillip C. Saunders, Christopher D. Yung, Michael Swaine, and Andrew Nien-Dzu Yang (Washington, DC: NDU Press, 2011), 198, http://ndupress.ndu.edu/Portals/68/Documents/Books/chinese-navy.pdf.
4. Office of Naval Intelligence (ONI), *The People's Liberation Army Navy: A Modern Navy with Chinese Characteristics* (Suitland, MD: ONI, August 2009), 5–6, www.fas.org/irp/agency/oni/pla-navy.pdf.

approach, China has elected (at least for the time being) to forgo development of a massive blue-water navy capable of challenging the United States directly. Instead, China is deploying a variety of systems and platforms, each designed to exploit areas of U.S. weakness. For example, China currently operates a large fleet of diesel-electric submarines which, because they are difficult to detect, can conduct surprise attacks on U.S. surface warships trying to gain access to contested waters.

The Role of the Fleet in China's Anti-Access Strategy

China's anti-access strategy does not rely exclusively on its naval power. Both China's air force, with its large inventory of multirole combat aircraft; and China's Second Artillery Corps, with its wide array of land-based ballistic and cruise missiles, are also expected to play important roles in carrying out this anti-access strategy. Nevertheless, the PLAN's increasingly capable surface combat ships will play a central role as well. China's growing fleet of heavily armed destroyers and frigates, complemented by large numbers of smaller surface vessels, such as corvettes and fast-attack craft, most of them armed with modern ASCMs, are designed to give the PLAN enormous striking power in a future struggle for access in the western Pacific. The striking power of the fleet is supplemented by an array of advanced ASCMs hosted on Chinese submarines and maritime aircraft.

The role of the PLAN's surface fleet in China's anti-access strategy is still evolving. While China has made significant progress in upgrading its fleet, it is still very much a work-in-progress. As yet, China's fleet remains outnumbered and outclassed by the U.S. Navy's advanced Arleigh Burke–class destroyers and Ticonderoga-class cruisers, complemented by capable frigates and other combat vessels. When U.S. aircraft carriers and nuclear attack submarines are factored into the mix, the U.S. Navy's advantage is overwhelming.

According to Rear Admiral Michael McDevitt, to counter the U.S. threat, China has opted for a two-tiered strategy, assigning different missions to its forces depending on the tier.[5] The inner tier or defensive zone (commonly referred to as the Near Seas) consists of the maritime waters extending out from China's coast to the First Island Chain, a distance of approximately 200 nautical miles, although it extends out somewhat farther to the north and south. The outer tier or defensive zone (Far Seas) includes the waters between the First and Second Island Chains, and extends out to a distance of between 1,200 and 1,300 nautical miles from China's coast.[6]

China's anti-access strategy requires Beijing to maintain much greater capability to operate in the Near Seas than in the Far Seas. Within the Near Seas, China must not only deny access to U.S. forces but also secure control of the seas in specified areas in the event

---

5. McDevitt, "PLA Navy's Antiaccess," 201–202.
6. Ibid.

The First and Second Island Chains

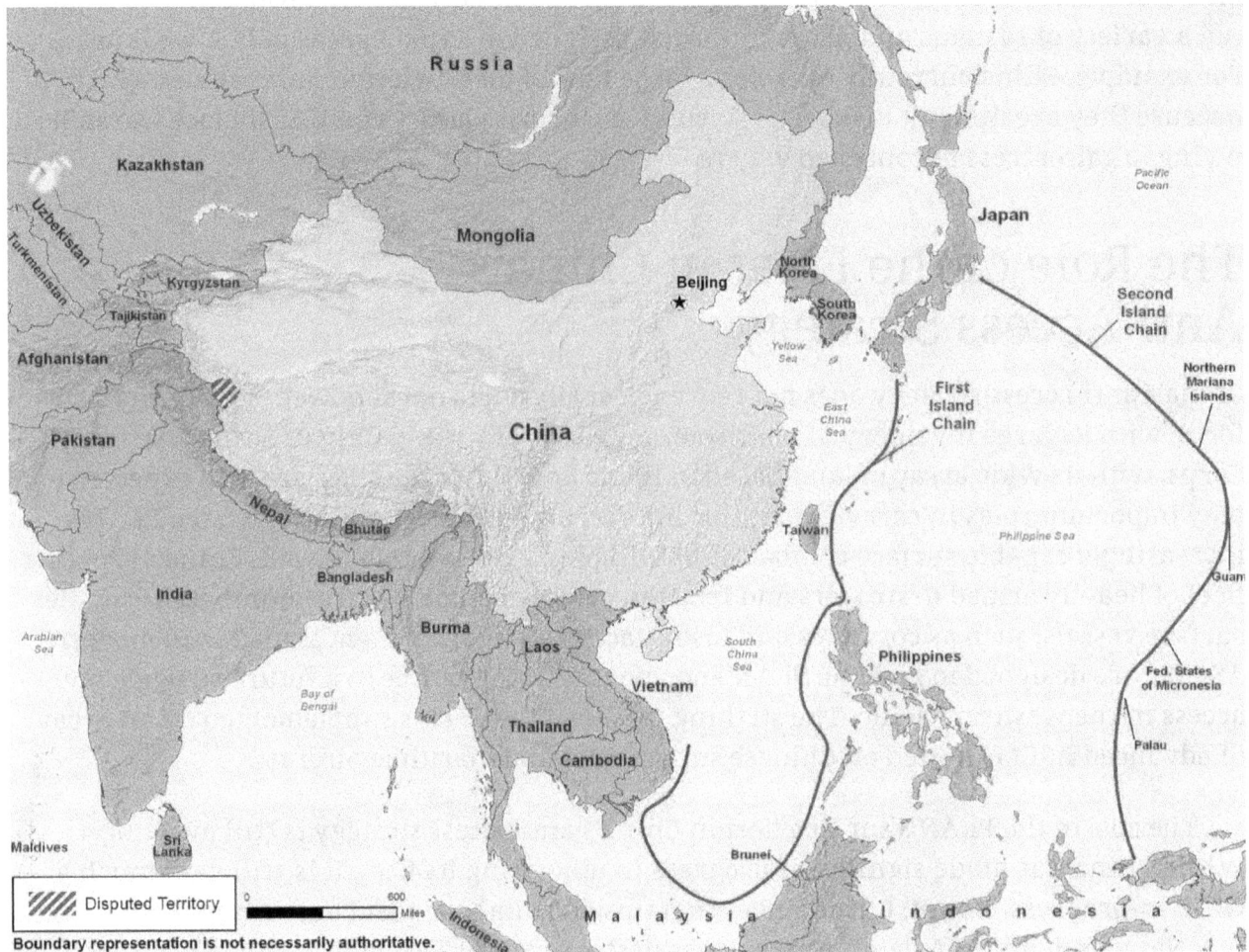

Source: Office of the Secretary of Defense, "Annual Report to Congress: Military and Security Developments Involving the People's Republic of China 2011," U.S. Department of Defense, 2011, 23, http://www.defense.gov/pubs/pdfs/2011 _CMPR_Final.pdf.

of conflict.[7] Maintaining local sea control will be crucial for achieving China's strategic objectives in most foreseeable conflict scenarios. For example, should China attempt to recover Taiwan by force, it not only must keep U.S. forces from intervening at the outset but also must seize local control of the Taiwan Strait and surrounding seas in order to conduct expeditionary operations against Taiwan itself, and it must maintain local control for the long term if it expects to hold on to Taiwan once it is taken.

Within the Far Seas defensive zone, however, China's mission is to be exclusively one of sea denial, at least for the near term. That means China must be able to hold U.S. forces at risk to prevent them from gaining control of the seas in that zone, although China need not control those seas itself.[8] In this case, the essential mission is to prevent U.S. Navy task

---

7. Ibid., 202.
8. Ibid.

forces from using the Far Seas as a safe bastion from which to launch long-range strikes against Chinese forces operating offshore or against the Chinese mainland.

Corresponding to these requirements, China's surface fleet is also expected to have different missions depending on the specific defensive zone involved. Within the Near Seas, the fleet will be expected to operate jointly with other PLA forces to deny U.S. warships access to these waters. China's fleet will also have to operate independently at significant distances from shore in order to seize and maintain local sea control. While long-range missiles, maritime aircraft, and submarines can be effective in preventing an opponent from gaining control of the seas in a contested area, they are incapable of gaining control of the seas on their own. For this mission, only surface warships will do, because they alone can provide the extended surface presence necessary to allow other military operations to take place. For example, surface warships are essential for conducting amphibious operations because only they can adequately protect troop transports and supply vessels transiting into the theater of operations.

Within the Far Seas, the role of China's surface fleet will remain limited to conducting occasional raids and engaging in long-range missile strikes to counter attempts by U.S. surface warships to operate in that zone. For the near term, however, the fleet will not be able to operate independently in the Far Seas for extended periods, as Chinese warships remain vulnerable to attack by U.S. combat aircraft, surface ships, and submarines. Eventually, however, as China adds blue-water capability, the surface fleet will increasingly be able to operate in the Far Seas as well. To achieve this objective, however, the PLAN will need to develop the kind of integrated battle groups long used by the U.S. Navy. Typically, such a battle group consists of a mix of surface warships, submarines, and other vessels, each having different competencies. For example, one vessel might specialize in naval air defense, while another focuses on anti-submarine warfare (ASW). In this way, the strengths of one ship are able to compensate for the weaknesses of others. Collectively, through the contributions of each ship, the battle group is able to maintain the full range of offensive and defensive combat capabilities needed to operate independently in the open oceans.[9]

While China eventually hopes to field a true blue-water navy, its fleet currently lacks the ships necessary to operate effectively in the open oceans. In fact, China's fleet is not yet capable of fulfilling many of the missions assigned to it by China's anti-access strategy, whether in the Near Seas or Far. Still, within a very short time, the fleet has made enormous progress in addressing key deficiencies and in improving its overall combat capabilities.

Until recently, China's surface fleet suffered from serious shortcomings in nearly every important combat category. For example, the fleet lacked the naval air defense capability necessary to operate safely outside the range of shore-based air defense systems, where ships would be highly vulnerable to U.S. air strikes. In addition, Chinese surface warships

---

9. Nan Li, "The Evolution of China's Naval Strategy and Capabilities: From 'Near Coast' and 'Near Seas' to 'Far Seas,'" in Saunders et al., *Chinese Navy*, 130.

had only limited ability to launch effective long-range missile strikes against enemy warships, leaving them at a distinct disadvantage when facing U.S. ships equipped with accurate, long-range anti-ship missiles. Finally, the fleet's ASW capability was extremely limited, leaving Chinese warships vulnerable to U.S. submarine attacks even when operating close to shore.

Given these shortcomings, until recently China has been forced to rely on other systems to implement its anti-access strategy. Within the First Island Chain, for example, China has relied primarily on its land-based combat aircraft, theater missile forces, and diesel submarines to conduct the bulk of its anti-access operations. Within the Second Island Chain, China has relied primarily on submarines and long-range missiles.

However, as the capabilities of China's surface fleet continue to develop, the situation is starting to change. While aircraft, missiles, and submarines will continue to play important roles in China's anti-access strategy, the role of China's surface fleet has been steadily increasing. Improved maritime strike capability has given Chinese warships a much greater chance of competing effectively against their U.S. counterparts. Likewise, improved naval air defense capability has given China's surface warships the ability to operate at increasingly greater distances from shore, as their dependence on shore-based air defense systems has declined. However, the fleet continues to suffer from limited ASW capabilities, and improvement in this area will be essential if the fleet hopes to gain the operational freedom needed to fulfill its anti-access missions.

The Need for Modern Military Equipment

At the time the new anti-access strategy was adopted, the PLAN was severely lacking in the kinds of advanced military systems needed to carry out the requisite operations. Due to its subordinate position to the army and its limited coastal defense mission, the PLAN was traditionally given low priority in China's defense budget. Consequently, the PLAN had been forced to rely on a collection of aging and relatively ineffective surface warships, submarines, and small attack craft, most of which were based on Soviet designs dating back to the early 1960s.[10] The PLAN was even more lacking in naval air power. Nor was China's air force able to fill the gap, because it lacked the necessary equipment to conduct effective maritime air operations due to its long-standing focus on providing air support for land operations. Correcting the PLAN's many deficiencies would require a complete overhaul of China's maritime forces, necessitating the purchase of new equipment and the development of suitable new concepts of operation.

The adoption of China's new strategy thus made it necessary to acquire a wide range of new platforms, sensors, and precision strike weapon systems for its maritime forces. Without such systems, China would be unable to effectively detect, track, and target U.S. aircraft and warships attempting to penetrate China's defensive perimeter. At the time the

---

10. Godwin, "PLA Faces Twenty-First Century," 39.

Annual Russian Arms Sales to China (1992–2014)

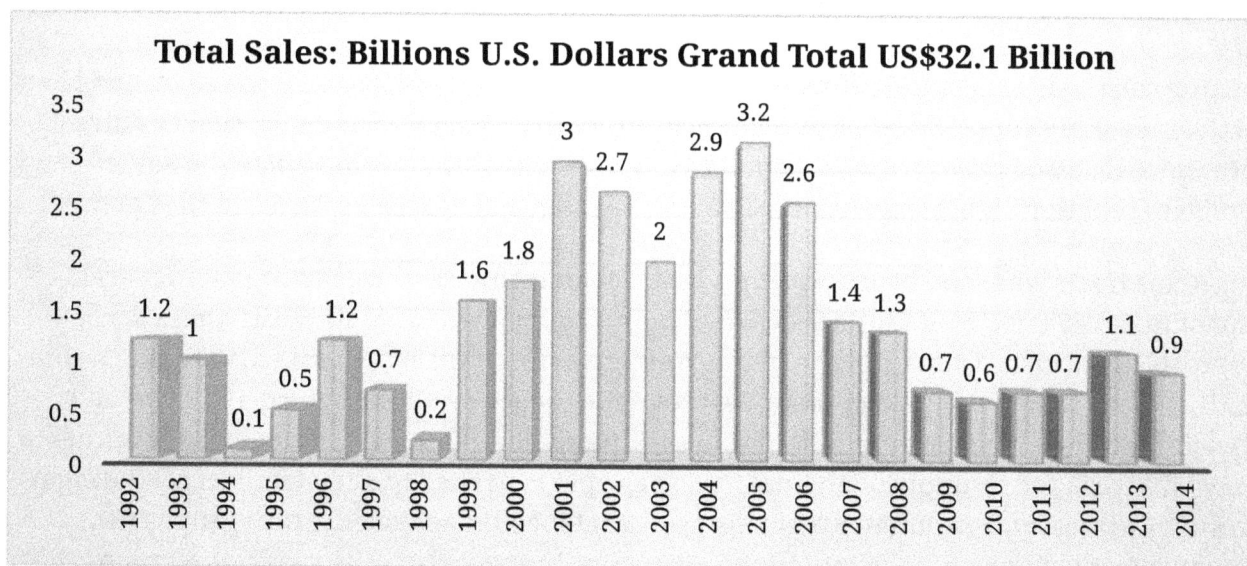

Total Sales: Billions U.S. Dollars Grand Total US$32.1 Billion

Year	Value
1992	1.2
1993	1
1994	0.1
1995	0.5
1996	1.2
1997	0.7
1998	0.2
1999	1.6
2000	1.8
2001	3
2002	2.7
2003	2
2004	2.9
2005	3.2
2006	2.6
2007	1.4
2008	1.3
2009	0.7
2010	0.6
2011	0.7
2012	0.7
2013	1.1
2014	0.9

Sources: SIPRI Arms Transfer Database; Linda Jakobsen, Paul Holtom, Dean Knox, and Jingchao Peng, *China's Energy and Security Relations with Russia: Hopes, Frustrations and Uncertainties* (Stockholm: SIPRI, October 2011), 14.

new strategy was adopted, however, China's defense industry seriously lacked the technical sophistication needed to produce these systems domestically. While China's leaders hoped to eventually modernize the defense industry, doing so would take considerable time and resources. Given the magnitude of the PLAN's many deficiencies, however, China's leaders decided that they could no longer wait for the defense industry to catch up, so they decided to look to foreign suppliers.[11]

For a variety of reasons, China turned to Russia as the principal source for the weapons needed to modernize its military. After the 1989 Tiananmen Square crackdown, the United States and most if its Western allies imposed a comprehensive arms embargo on China. Fortunately for China, Russia soon emerged as a satisfactory alternative. Not only was Russia willing to sell China the kinds of advanced systems that it needed, China was already quite familiar with Russian equipment, having had long experience with Russian systems dating back to the Sino-Soviet alliance of the 1950s. For its part, Russia had its own reasons for wanting to reestablish the arms-trading relationship. During the economic crisis that followed the collapse of the Soviet Union, Russia's defense industries found themselves virtually cut off from state funding as orders from the Russian military almost entirely dried up. To survive, they were forced to turn to the export markets. The possibility of renewed arms sales to China was therefore seen as especially timely and welcome. This confluence of circumstances provided the impetus for resumption of large-scale arms transfers from Russia to China in 1991, a process that continues to this day.

---

11. Bates Gill, "China's Newest Warships," *Far Eastern Economic Review* 163, no. 4 (January 27, 2000): 30.

There were political reasons for the resumption of the arms trading relationship as well. For China, the renewal of arms trade with Russia was part of a broader strategic agenda. After Tiananmen, China's relations with the West deteriorated, leaving Beijing feeling relatively isolated. Fortunately for Beijing, Soviet leader Mikhail Gorbachev had been actively seeking at that time to improve relations with China as part of his broader outreach program. He also hoped that a reduction in tensions with China would allow the Soviet Union to reduce military expenditures needed to maintain a large presence in the Far East.

Arms trade was seen by both parties as a way to reinforce the growing political relationship. Russia saw that China's leaders deeply appreciated Russia's willingness to continue to sell arms to China in spite of the Western arms embargo. Russia also realized that selling arms to China would create a certain dependence on China's part, and even give Russia some level of influence over China's military. For example, China would continue to rely on Russia for resupply of engines and spare parts needed to keep transferred Russian military aircraft operational. Russia also saw that it could achieve certain geopolitical benefits from supporting the buildup of China's military forces. The kinds of weapons that Russia was providing were geared much more toward fighting a maritime conflict with the West than a future land campaign against Russia. In fact, Moscow hoped that the buildup of China's maritime forces might intensify the growing competition between China and the United States in the western Pacific, leaving the two strategically focused more on each other and away from Russia. Finally, over time, both realized that their principal strategic focus increasingly pointed in other directions. While China's focus lay squarely on the western Pacific, Russia was more concerned about NATO expansion into Eastern Europe. Consequently, each saw the benefit of having a demilitarized area on their border that could serve as a quiet strategic rear, allowing them both to focus on their respective areas of primary interest.

3 | Russian Defense Assistance Programs

Russian Naval Vessels and Related Contributions

Since the Cold War, Russia has been instrumental in helping China to improve the quality and capability of its surface combat fleet. During this time, Russia has engaged in large-scale arms sales, delivering sophisticated destroyers, advanced weapon systems, radar systems, and various components that have been incorporated into indigenous Chinese weapons. Russia has also provided critical technical assistance, including technology transfer and engineering support, to help China to develop a number of domestically produced surface warships, weapon systems, and components and to aid China in the development of its domestic shipbuilding industry.

SOVREMENNY-CLASS DESTROYERS

In 1997, China purchased two Sovremenny-class (Project 956E) destroyers from Russia for a reported cost of US$800 million.[1] In 2002, the PLAN ordered two more Sovremenny destroyers in a deal valued at US$1.4 billion, but this time they ordered the more advanced Project 956EM models.[2] The Sovremenny is a conventionally powered multipurpose missile destroyer, developed during the late-Soviet era. It is designed primarily for anti-surface warfare operations, air defense, and coastal bombardment, although it possesses limited ASW capabilities as well.[3]

The Sovremennys are equipped with advanced 3M-80E (SS-N-22) Sunburn (aka Moskit) ASCMs, although the last two ships came with the even more advanced 3M-80MVE version of the Sunburn. The original version has a range of 120 km, while the later version has an extended range of up to 240 km.[4] The Sunburn was designed specifically to defeat the U.S.

---

1. Richard D. Fisher, Jr., "Foreign Arms Acquisition and PLA Modernization," in *China's Military Faces the Future*, ed. James R. Lilley and David Shambaugh (Washington, DC: M.E. Sharpe, 1999), 103.

2. Dennis M. Gormley, Andrew S. Erickson, and Jingdong Yuan, *A Low-Visibility Force Multiplier: Assessing China's Cruise Missile Ambitions* (Washington, DC: National Defense University Press, 2014), 45, http://ndupress .ndu.edu/Portals/68/Documents/Books/force-multiplier.pdf; "Hangzou Type 957 Sov-Sovremenny," globalsecurity.org, http://www.globalsecurity.org/military/world/china/haizhou.htm.

3. "From Sovremenny to Gremyashchy: The Sovremenny Class Destroyers," *Jane's Intelligence Review*, September 1, 1989.

4. Gormley et al., *Force Multiplier*, 19.

Sovremenny-Class Destroyer

Source: U.S. Navy via Wikimedia Commons, https://commons.wikimedia.org/wiki/File:Gremyashchiy.jpg.

Aegis combat system, which provides area air defense coverage for U.S. Navy ships against aircraft and incoming cruise missiles.[5] It is a supersonic missile, and can achieve speeds of up to Mach 3.0.[6] It flies at a sea-skimming altitude of just seven meters as it approaches the target.[7] During the final approach, it can reportedly execute 15g terminal maneuvers to evade ship-borne point defense systems.[8]

The Sunburn's combination of high speed, low altitude, and great maneuverability leaves little time for defenders to react before the missile strikes. Collectively, these capabilities make the Sunburn one of the world's most formidable ASCMs. In fact, several analysts have questioned whether existing U.S. ship self-defense systems are up to the task of defeating them.[9]

---

5. See Sergey Sokut, "Moskit Versus Aegis," *Moscow Nezavisimoye Voyennoye Obozreniye*, March 24, 2000, FBIS Document ID: CEP20000404000293, April 4, 2000.

6. Carlo Kopp, "Soviet/Russian Cruise Missiles," *Air Power Australia*, Technical Report APA-TR-2009-0805, last updated April 2012, http://www.ausairpower.net/APA-Rus-Cruise-Missiles.html.

7. Kopp, "Soviet/Russian Cruise Missiles"; Steven J. Zaloga, "Russia's Moskit Anti-Ship Missile," *Jane's Intelligence Review*, April 1996.

8. Zaloga, "Russia's Moskit."

9. Ibid.

The SS-N-22 Sunburn (Raduga P-270 Moskit) Missile

Source: Wikimedia Commons, https://commons.wikimedia.org/wiki/File:Moskit_missile.jpg.

Onboard targeting is handled by the Sovremenny's powerful Russian-built Band Stand (Mineral ME) radar. Band Stand reportedly provides over-the-horizon (OTH) search capability to detect and track enemy warships at a range of up to 250 km in active radar mode and 450 km in passive radar mode.[10] The Sovremenny can also reportedly receive OTH targeting data from other naval vessels, and from reconnaissance aircraft and helicopters. Reportedly, the ship can also deliver updates to the missile while it is in flight via a data link.[11]

For air defense, the Sovremenny destroyers are equipped with two SA-N-7 Uragan (Gadfly) medium-range, surface-to-air missile batteries.[12] The Gadfly is a naval version

---

10. James Bussert, "China Copies Russian Ship Technology for Use and Profit," *Signal Magazine*, June 2008, http://www.afcea.org/content/?q=china-copies-russian-ship-technology-use-and-profit.

11. Zaloga, "Russia's Moskit."

12. "From Sovremenny." Although some sources credit the Sovremenny with having the SA-N-12 Grizzly air defense system, a 2009 Office of Naval Intelligence Report states that all of them are equipped with the SA-N-7 Gadfly. See ONI, *People's Liberation Army Navy*, 18. This is confirmed by *Jane's Fighting Ships 2014–2015*. But compare: One source suggests that the later Sovremenny destroyers were equipped with the 9K37M1-2 Shtil (SA-N-12 "Grizzly") air defense system. Gordon Arthur, "Keeping the Enemy at Bay—Warship Anti-Missile Defence," *Defence Review Asia*, May 6, 2013, http://www.defencereviewasia.com/articles/219/KEEPING-THE-ENEMY-AT-BAY-WARSHIP-ANTI-MISSILE-DEFENCE.

of the land-based SA-11 Buk missile system, itself a variant of the system believed to have been used to down Malaysian Airlines Flight 17 over Ukraine in mid-2014. At the time of delivery, the Gadfly was one of the most formidable air defense platforms in production, and compared favorably with the Standard Missile system hosted on U.S. Aegis combat ships. The Gadfly can strike targets at a range of 25 km and at an altitude of up to 46,000 feet.[13]

The SA-N-7 Gadfly relies on the Russian-built Top Plate (Fregat MAE-3) air surveillance radar for search and detection of aerial targets. It is designed to detect and identify aerial targets at a range of up to 180 km for aircraft and up to 40 km for sea-skimming missiles.[14] It can also reportedly detect targets at altitudes of up to 98,000 feet.[15] The Top Plate is intended to operate in conditions of intense electronic warfare, employing sophisticated electronic countermeasures to neutralize attempts at jamming and deception. Targets identified by the Top Plate are then cued to the SA-N-7's Front Dome (MR-90 Orekh) fire control radar system, another Russian-built system. The Front Dome's mission is to target enemy aircraft and incoming cruise missiles, and to guide the Gadfly's missiles to their targets.

At the time of purchase, the Sovremenny destroyers were far and away the best ships in China's navy and their purchase remedied several shortcomings. Most notably, the Sunburn-armed Sovremenny substantially increased striking power against other surface warships.[16] Not only did the Sunburn missile provide the PLAN for the first time with a long-range precision strike capability, but its supersonic speed and high maneuverability gave it great penetrating power against even the most sophisticated ship defense systems.

Furthermore, the Sovremennys were the first ships to provide China's fleet with a real, albeit limited, area air defense capability. Prior to their purchase, the PLAN had historically suffered from a lack of effective air defense capability.[17] The Legacy HQ-7 Crotale system, for example, had a range of just 14 km. With a range of 25 km, the Sovremenny's SA-N-7 Gadfly gave China significantly increased air defense coverage against a variety of aerial targets.[18] While a substantial improvement over the Crotale, the Gadfly's limited range was still insufficient by modern standards.

---

13. "The Sovremenny Destroyer," *Jane's Fighting Ships: 2014–2015*, 137; "The Sovremenny Destroyer," *Jane's Fighting Ships: 2004–2005*, 609.

14. "Fregat-MAE Series Surveillance Radars," *Jane's C4ISR & Mission Systems: Maritime*, February 2, 2015; "Fregat MAE-3," Deagal.com, http://www.deagel.com/Ship-Sensors/Fregat-MAE-3_a001879004.aspx; Kerry Plowright, "China Files: People's Liberation Army Navy Ships," Fact Sheet ADF Weapons Brief 2008, 14, http://www.vostokstation.com.au/PLAN_Ships.pdf.

15. "Fregat-MAE," *Jane's C4ISR*.

16. Li, "China's Naval Strategy," 121.

17. Neil Andrew Harmon, "Russian Conventional Arms Transfers Since 1991: Implications for U.S. Naval Forces" (master's thesis, Naval Postgraduate School, 2001), 50, http://www.dtic.mil/docs/citations/ADA391987. *U.S. Department of Defense, Annual Report to Congress: Military Power of the People's Republic of China 2004* (Washington, DC: Office of the Secretary of Defense, 2004), 36 (hereafter, the short form of each such annual report is cited as *DOD China Report* followed by applicable year of publication).

18. ONI, *People's Liberation Army Navy*, 18.

Close-up of Front Dome (MR-90 Orekh) Fire Control Radar

Source: Admiral Hood via Wikimedia Commons, https://commons.wikimedia.org/wiki/File:D61_INS_Delhi_MR-90
_Orekh_Illuminator_Vladivostok_20011-04-19.jpg.

OTHER CONTRIBUTIONS TO CHINESE SURFACE WARSHIP DESIGN

Excluding the Sovremenny, China has elected to build all of its own surface warships in recent years. In fact, Chinese shipyards have become quite adept at using modular construction methods to build modern naval vessels. With important exceptions described below, these new Chinese vessels are also equipped for the most part with indigenously developed systems. Nevertheless, Russia has contributed in important ways to the development of China's shipbuilding capabilities and, in at least one case, in the specific design of one of China's latest warships. A report published by the U.S. Defense Threat Reduction Agency noted, for example, that "like many Chinese military systems, [China's indigenous] destroyers lean heavily on technology and design expertise acquired through Russian arms sales."[19] Another source reported that "Russia's Severnoye design firm has played

---

19. Dallas Boyd, *Advanced Technology Acquisition Strategies of the People's Republic of China*, Defense Threat Reduction Agency Report No. ASCO 2010 021, September 2010, 19, http://fas.org/irp/agency/dod/dtra /strategies.pdf.

an important role in the design of the Type 054A [Jiangkai II] frigate [further described below], largely due to the extensive Russian systems installed."[20]

Russian Weapon Systems, Components, and Related Technology

While thus far the Sovremenny destroyers are the only complete naval ships provided by Russia since the Cold War, Russia has also contributed to the development of the PLAN's surface warfare systems in other important ways. Chief among these has been Russia's provision of a number of components and key weapon systems currently used by China's surface combat fleet and its other maritime forces. Russia has also provided substantial technology assistance and engineering support for China's fleet.

ASCM SYSTEMS

Over the last 20 years, Russia has assisted China's cruise missile program in two important ways. First, Russia has transferred a number of advanced Russian cruise missiles, along with highly capable radar systems able to detect, track, and target enemy warships at sea. Russia has also provided substantial technology assistance for China's own cruise missile programs.

Provision of Russian ASCMs

Outright transfer of Russian ASCMs has been one of the most important means by which China has upgraded its ASCM capabilities. As already noted, China acquired highly capable, ship-launched Sunburn ASCMs through its purchase of Sovremenny destroyers from Russia. Russia has also transferred several other advanced ASCMs to China.

These missiles include the widely feared 3M-54E Klub (SS-N-27B Sizzler), which China received when it purchased Kilo-class submarines from Russia, at an estimated cost of $1.6 billion, in 2002.[21] The 3M-54E Klub Sizzler is part of a family of Klub missiles, which also includes subsonic anti-ship and land-attack variants. The 3M-54E Klub Sizzler is an advanced anti-ship missile with a range of up to 220 km.[22] During most of its flight path, the missile flies at subsonic speed, to conserve fuel. Once the target is acquired, however, the 3M-54E Klub Sizzler accelerates to speeds of up to Mach 2.9 for a final sprint to the target at a sea-skimming altitude of just 15 feet above sea level.[23] It can also reportedly employ violent end-stage maneuvers to defeat interceptors. All of these measures make it very difficult to intercept.

---

20. Keith Jacobs, "PLA-Navy Update: People's Liberation Army-Navy Military Technical Developments," *Naval Forces* 28, no. 1 (2007): 26.

21. John Pomfret, "China to Buy 8 More Russian Submarines," *Washington Post*, June 25, 2002, http://www.washingtonpost.com/archive/politics/2002/06/25/china-to-buy-8-more-russian-submarines/eaec2e3e-fe7a-47a4-ba29-ac42a18f60bb/; Gormley et al., *Force Multiplier*, xix.

22. *DOD China Report 2015*, 10.

23. Carlo Kopp, "Precision Guided Munitions in the Region," *Air Power Australia*, Technical Report APA-TR-2007-0109, last updated August 2009, http://www.ausairpower.net/APA-Regional-PGM.html.

SS-N-27 (3M-54E) "Sizzler"

Source: Allocer via Wikimedia Commons, https://commons.wikimedia.org/wiki/File:3M-54E_missile_MAKS2009.jpg.

Russia also transferred to China both the Kh-31A (active radar) and the Kh-31P (anti-radiation) air-launched cruise missiles. Both variants can be used in an anti-ship capacity. According to its manufacturer, the Kh-31A has an effective range of up to 70 km (110 km for the Kh-31P), and can achieve speeds of up to Mach 3.0.[24] The Kh-31A can be launched from a variety of aircraft, but according to the U.S. Department of Defense, the Chinese will deploy the missile primarily on Su-30MK2 combat aircraft previously purchased from Russia.[25] This missile's "combination of high speed, small size and long range makes it a challenging target to intercept by air defences."[26] China currently produces the Kh-31P under license from Russia, although the Chinese version is designated the YJ-91.

Finally, in the early 2000s, Russia developed a custom version of its Kh-59 air-launched cruise missile for China. The missile was designed specifically for use on Russian Su-30MKK aircraft purchased by Beijing and specifically to serve in an anti-ship role. The customized Kh-59MK is a long-range missile, which can strike targets at up to 285 km.[27] These capabilities make it ideal for launching standoff attacks against enemy warships. It flies at subsonic speeds of around Mach 0.9, and is capable of approaching the target at a sea-skimming altitude of just seven meters above sea level.[28]

---

24. "Kh-31A Medium-range Anti-ship Airborne Missile," Tactical Missiles Corporation Website, http://eng .ktrv.ru/production_eng/323/512/370/; "Kh-31P—Airborne Guided Missile," Tactical Missiles Corporation Website, http://eng.ktrv.ru/production_eng/323/511/371/; "Kh-31A," Deagel.com, http://www.deagel.com /Anti-Ship-Missiles/Kh-31A_a001028002.aspx; "Kh-31P," Deagel.com, http://www.deagel.com/Anti-Radiation -Missiles/Kh-31P_a001028001.aspx.

25. *DOD China Report 2011*, 32.

26. Carlo Kopp, "Soviet/Russian Tactical Air-to-Surface Missiles," *Air Power Australia*, Technical Report APA-TR-2009-0804, last updated April 2012, http://www.ausairpower.net/APA-Rus-ASM.html.

27. Kopp, "Tactical Air-to-Surface Missiles."

28. "Kh-59MK Airborne Guided Missile," Tactical Missiles Corporation Website, http://eng.ktrv.ru /production_eng/323/512/517/.

Kh-31A (Active Radar) Missile

Source: Vitaly V. Kuzmin via Wikimedia Commons, https://commons.wikimedia.org/wiki/File:International_Maritime
_Defence_Show_2011_(375-73).jpg.

Derivatives of Russian ASCMs

Recently, China has started developing a new generation of supersonic ASCMs, which all appear to be copies (or derivatives) of previously transferred Russian ASCMs. For example, China recently introduced a new missile, referred to as the YJ-18, which is reportedly a copy of the Russian 3M-54E Klub Sizzler missile.[29] It reportedly has an effective range of up to 180 km.[30] Like the 3M-54E Klub Sizzler, the YJ-18 travels initially at subsonic speed but accelerates to speeds of up to Mach 3.0 as it approaches the target.[31] This unusual characteristic is a strong indicator of its Russian heritage. In its 2015 report, the U.S. Office of Naval Intelligence confirmed that the YJ-18 has now been deployed on the Type 052D

---

29. Dennis M. Gormley, Andrew S. Erickson, and Jingdong Yuan "A Potent Vector: Assessing Chinese Cruise Missile Developments," *Joint Force Quarterly*, 4th Quarter Issue, September 30, 2014, 102, http://ndupress.ndu .edu/Media/News/NewsArticleView/tabid/7849/Article/11240/jfq-75-a-potent-vector-assessing-chinese-cruise -missile-developments.aspx. See also Richard D. Fisher, Jr., "Updated: Zhuhai Surprise: China's Third 'Russian' Supersonic ASCM," *Aviation Week*, November 7, 2014, http://aviationweek.com/blog/updated-zhuhai-surprise -china-s-third-russian-supersonic-ascm.

30. Gormley et al., "Potent Vector," 102. Note, however, that the latest DOD report on China's military cites the YJ-18's range at a staggering 535km. If true, this would represent an enormous increase in China's long-range anti-ship striking power. *DOD China Report 2015*, 10.

31. Gormley et al., "Potent Vector," 102.

Kh-59 *Ovod* (AS-13 "Kingbolt") Missile

Source: Allocer via Wikimedia Commons, https://commons.wikimedia.org/wiki/File:Kh-59MK2_maks2009.jpg.

Chinese Luyang III destroyer, while a submarine-launched variant either is or will soon be deployed on Chinese Song-, Yuan-, and Shang-class submarines.[32]

In addition, China has been developing another supersonic ASCM known as the YJ-12. This new missile is reportedly based upon the Russian Kh-31. The "YJ-12 appears to be a considerably lengthened Russian Kh-31–type missile and is speculated to have a range of 250 km and a speed of Mach 2.5."[33] Like the Kh-31 from which it was apparently derived, the YJ-12 is expected to be an air-launched missile. According to the U.S. Department of Defense, the YJ-12 is "capable of being launched from [Chinese] H-6 bombers"[34] although it is unclear whether it has actually been deployed at this time.

Finally, according to a recent report, the Chinese are developing another missile, designated the CX-1, which was exhibited at the 2014 Zhuhai airshow. The CX-1 was described as a new Chinese supersonic ASCM.[35] Wang Hongpo, the CX-1's designer, told a Chinese military journalist that the missile "has a range of 280 kilometers, can attain a speed of Mach 3 and is capable of sinking a large warship. The missile lowers its altitude to 10 meters when it arrives at a distance 10 kilometers away from its target."[36]

---

32. Office of Naval Intelligence (ONI), *The PLA Navy: New Capabilities and Missions for the 21st Century* (Suitland, MD: ONI, 2015), 16, 19.
33. Gormley et al., "Potent Vector," 102. See also Fisher, "Zhuhai Surprise."
34. *DOD China Report 2015*, 46.
35. Fisher, "Zhuhai Surprise."
36. "CX-1 Supersonic Cruise Missile Exhibited at Zhuhai Air Show," *Want China Times*, November 16, 2014, http://www.wantchinatimes.com/news-subclass-cnt.aspx?id=20141116000138&cid=1101.

P-800 Oniks/Yakhont Missile, from Which CX-1 Is Reportedly Derived

Source: Flickr user Times Asi, https://www.flickr.com/photos/94141246@N05/15709747667/in/photolist-pWdyEp.

However, the new missile looks very similar to the Brahmos ASCM, which was codeveloped by Russia and India. The two missiles "share the distinctive cone-inlet air intake, a two-stage structure and similar dimensions."[37] The Brahmos itself is based on Russia's highly regarded P-800 Oniks (Yakhont) supersonic ASCM. The CX-1 missile also reportedly shares similar performance parameters as the Yakhont. If the report is true, however, the means by which China may have copied the Brahmos (or Yakhont) remains a mystery, because there are no confirmed reports of a prior sale, and presumably India would have never authorized such a sale to a country it regards as a strategic rival.

At any rate, the addition of supersonic YJ-12, YJ-18, and CX-1 ASCMs in the Chinese inventory is an ominous new development for the naval balance in the western Pacific. Until now, China's fleet has relied primarily on older, less capable ASCMs, such as the YJ-62 and YJ-83. As these missiles are replaced by newer, more sophisticated missiles, like the YJ-12, the PLAN's striking power will be increased enormously.

Provision of Russian ASCM Systems and Technology

In addition to transferring advanced ASCMs outright, Russia has provided China with substantial technical assistance for its indigenous cruise missile programs. Much of this

---

37. Fisher, "Zhuhai Surprise."

assistance is of a general nature, having broad applicability for both China's anti-ship and land-attack cruise missile programs. According to a recent report sponsored by the National Defense University (NDU), for example, Russian technicians have been previously retained to work on Chinese cruise missile programs.[38] In 1992, *Kommersant* reported that "China . . . is currently acquiring from Russia missile guidance technology, T-72 tanks, rocket motors, and S-300 surface-to-air missiles."[39] During the 1990s, China also reportedly purchased missile-guidance and rocket technology from Russia.[40] The same NDU-sponsored study stated that "it is clear that China continues to rely on foreign, and in particular Russian, technology, for development of cruise missiles."[41]

This is not to say that China is wholly dependent on Russia for advanced cruise missile technology. In fact, in recent years, China has demonstrated a growing independence from Russia in this area. Most importantly, Chinese surface warships (excluding the Sovremenny) now rely almost exclusively on indigenously developed ASCMs, especially the YJ-83 and YJ-62.[42] These systems have evolved from earlier Chinese designs and are quite capable in their own right. Nevertheless, advanced Russian ASCMs like the Sunburn and the 3M-54E Klub Sizzler (and perhaps the new Russian derivatives, such as the YJ-18) still constitute the best-performing cruise missiles in China's inventory in terms of their total package of high speed, long range, and great penetrating capability. Moreover, China's surface warships still rely heavily on Russian ship-based radar systems for acquisition and targeting of enemy warships. This is especially true for China's latest and most effective warships, including the Luzhou-class and Luyang-class destroyers, as well as the Jiangkai II frigate.[43]

Impact of Russian ASCM Support

In general, then, Russian ASCMs, advanced radar systems, and related technology have given China's anti-ship precision strike capability a real boost. Russian military assistance has yielded improvements in intelligence, surveillance, and reconnaissance (ISR), in terms of enhanced surface search, tracking, and targeting capability; as well as in anti-ship missile capability, in terms of increased range, speed, penetrating capability, and ultimately sheer striking power.

China's fleet also continues to use sophisticated Russian radar systems like the Band Stand to provide acquisition and targeting for its anti-ship missile systems. The Band Stand represents a significant upgrade for the PLAN's cruise missile targeting capability. The U.S. Office of Naval Intelligence recently cited "[t]he use of shipboard helicopters, the [Band Stand] Mineral-ME radar, and datalinks" as important factors contributing to the PLAN's upgraded capability to engage surface warships, because of their enhanced targeting

---

38. Gormley et al., *Force Multiplier*, 13.

39. Pavel Popov and Georgii Bovt, "Russian Military Hardware to Be Shipped to China," *Kommersant Daily*, November 20, 1992, 8, in FBIS-SOV-92-226, 23 November 1992.

40. Elizabeth Wishnick, *Mending Fences: The Evolution of Moscow's China Policy from Brezhnev to Yeltsin* (Seattle: University of Washington Press, 2001), 144.

41. Gormley et al., *Force Multiplier*, 10.

42. See generally *Jane's Fighting Ships: 2014–2015*, 136–144.

43. Ibid.

Chinese Type 054A Jiangkai II Frigate Equipped with Band Stand Radar

capability.[44] Without such systems, China would have had to make do with inferior legacy systems, which would have left it at a disadvantage in the battle for situational awareness that dominates today's naval battlespace.

Likewise, China has gained much through its acquisition and deployment of sophisticated Russian ASCMs. Prior to China's acquisition of the first pair of Russian Sovremenny destroyers in 1997, the range of the PLAN's ASCMs remained quite limited. China's acquisition of Russian Sunburn and 3M-54E Klub Sizzler missiles represented a significant increase in long-range strike capability. Prior to their acquisition, "the subsonic YJ-8A had the longest range of any ASCM in the PLA(N) inventory at ~65 [nautical miles]," [45] although later Chinese missiles, such as the YJ-62/83 missiles, were also comparable to the extended-range Russian missiles.

---

44. ONI, *People's Liberation Army Navy*, 18.
45. Ibid., 27–28.

Anti-Ship Missiles Acquired Outright from Russia or Derived from Russian Technology

Class	Manufacturer	Launch Platform	Range	Speed
SS-N-22 Sunburn	Russia	Ship	240 km	Supersonic
SS-N-27B Klub (Sizzler)	Russia	Submarine	220 km	Supersonic
Kh-31 Krypton	Russia	Aircraft	70–110 km	Supersonic
Kh-59MK Kingbolt	Russia	Aircraft	285 km	Subsonic
YJ-12	China	Aircraft	250 km	Supersonic
YJ-18	China	Ship, submarine	180 km	Supersonic
CX-1	China	Unknown	280 km	Supersonic

Sources: Kopp, "Soviet/Russian Cruise Missiles"; Kopp, "Tactical Air-to-Surface Missiles"; "Kh-31A/P Medium-range Anti-ship Airborne Missile," Tactical Missiles Corporation; Gormley et al., *Force Multiplier*, 19; Gormley et al., "Potent Vector," 102; Fisher, "Zhuhai Surprise."

Russian ASCMs also exhibit superior speed and penetrating capability when compared with their Chinese counterparts. The Sunburn, 3M-54E Klub Sizzler, Kh-31A, and Kh-31P ASCMs all fly at supersonic speeds in excess of Mach 2.0, and in some cases up to Mach 3.0. By contrast, the majority of China's indigenous ASCMs all operate at subsonic speed. In fact, China has just started deploying supersonic ASCMs, and even these are apparently based on Russian designs.[46] Russian ASCMs are also more accurate and more maneuverable than their Chinese counterparts, and they possess the ability to fly at sea-skimming altitudes.

In the competition between ASCMs and naval air defense systems, superior speed and penetrating power are crucial. Consequently, Russian missiles like the Sunburn and the 3M-54E Klub Sizzler and perhaps the new YJ-12/18 Russian derivatives offer China its best opportunity to penetrate sophisticated Western anti-ship defense systems. Moreover, China's Russian-built ASCMs include a range of air-launched, surface-launched, and submarine-launched models. Collectively, these provide China with the ability to attack U.S. surface warships from multiple directions and platforms, greatly complicating the task of the defender.

NAVAL AIR DEFENSE SYSTEMS

As the U.S. Office of Naval Intelligence noted in its 2009 report on Chinese naval capabilities, Beijing has made significant strides in improving its fleet air-defense capability.[47] By contributing a number of advanced air defense platforms, Russia has been vital to this effort. Moscow has also provided technology assistance, which has allowed China to develop several advanced air defense systems indigenously. Collectively, Russian air defense technology has enabled China's fleet to make rapid advances in overcoming its lack of naval air defense capability, a long-standing weakness of China's navy.

---

46. Gormley et al., "Potent Vector," 102.
47. ONI, *People's Liberation Army Navy*, 18.

Provision of Russian Air Defense Systems

Aside from the purchase of the Sovremenny destroyer, among the first steps taken in 2004 was to equip China's Luyang I–class (Type 052B) destroyers with the Russian SA-N-12 Shtil 9M38M2 (Grizzly) air defense system.[48] Deployment of the SA-N-12 represented a substantial increase in performance over the SA-N-7 Gadfly installed on the Sovremenny destroyers. The new SA-N-12 offered improved capability against incoming cruise and ballistic missiles. It also had an increased range of up to 35 km, an incremental increase over the Gadfly's 25 km range. The SA-N-12 was also able to strike targets at higher altitudes of up to 75,000 feet, compared with 46,000 for the Gadfly. Like the Sovremenny, the Luyang I relies on the Top Plate radar system for surveillance and tracking and the Front Dome for missile guidance. The addition of the SA-N-7 and the SA-N-12 provided China with its first true mid-range area air defense capability.

China also began deploying the Russian SA-N-20 (S-300PMU) Gargoyle (Rif-M Fort) on Chinese Luzhou-class (Type 051C) destroyers, when they were first commissioned in 2004.[49] The SA-N-20 is the naval variant of Russia's formidable land-based SA-20 air defense system. It is equipped with the 48N6, a versatile missile, capable of striking a variety of aerial targets at ranges of up to 150 km and at altitudes of up to 90,000 feet.[50] The SA-N-20 gave China its first true long-range area air defense capability. That China chose a Russian air defense system for the Luzhou, whose chief mission is air defense, is particularly important as an example of China's continuing reliance on Russian technology in the vital field of wide-area air defense.

Like the Sovremenny, the Luzhou also uses the Russian Top Plate (Fregat MAE-3) surveillance radar for detection and tracking of aerial targets. However, the Luzhou uses a different fire control radar, the Russian SA-N-20's Tomb Stone radar system. This radar system is designed to track and target enemy aircraft and other aerial targets at a range of between 200 and 300 km.[51] The Tomb Stone also provides midcourse guidance and terminal phase illumination for the SA-N-20's 48N6 missile.[52] According to data compiled by Kerry Plowright, "[t]he radar can direct 12 missiles to engage 6 targets simultaneously."[53]

Chinese Derivatives of Russian Air Defense Systems

In addition to purchasing Russian air defense systems, China has also used Russian air defense technology to produce its own family of medium- and long-range naval air defense systems. For example, China's Luyang II–class (Type 052C) destroyers are

---

48. "The Type 052B Destroyer," *Jane's Fighting Ships: 2014–2015*, 138.

49. ONI, *People's Liberation Army Navy*, 18.

50. "Luzhou-Class," *Jane's Fighting Ships: 2014–2015*, 136.

51. Nikolaos Diakadis, *An Assessment of China's Defense Strategy in the Post-Cold War Era: What Role for Bilateral Defense Cooperation with Russia?* (Piraeus, Greece: December 2009), 193, http://www.isn.ethz.ch/Digital-Library/Publications/Detail/?lang=en&id=120473.

52. David Barton, "Design of the S-300P and S-300V Surface-to-Air Missile Systems," *Air Power Australia*, March 2009.

53. Plowright, "China Files," 26.

The SA-N-12 Shtil "Grizzly" Missile, Mounted Here on an Indian Navy Frigate

Source: Wikimedia Commons, https://commons.wikimedia.org/wiki/File:Indian-navy-missile.jpg.

currently equipped with the HHQ-9 air defense system. The HHQ-9 is the naval version of China's land-based HQ-9 air defense system. According to Carlo Kopp, "[t]here is general agreement in open sources that the HQ-9 uses Russian S-300PMU technology extensively."[54] The S-300PMU is widely regarded as one of the most capable air defense

54. Carlo Kopp, "CPMIEC HQ-9 / HHQ-9 / FD-2000 / FT-2000 Self-Propelled Air Defence System," *Air Power Australia*, Technical Report APA-TR-2009-1103, last updated April 2012, http://www.ausairpower.net/APA-HQ-9 -FD-FT-2000.html. More specifically, in the same report, Dr. Kopp indicates that the technology is derived from the SA-10C Grumble variant of the S-300PMU family of air defense systems.

systems in the world.[55] The missile fired by the HHQ-9 appears to be nearly identical to the S-300's 48N6 missile as well.[56] Some analysts even assert that China engaged Russian missile maker Almaz-Antey to codevelop the HQ-9.[57] The HHQ-9 was designed to provide long-range area air defense for the fleet, and it is reportedly capable of striking a variety of targets at distances of up to 100 km.[58] HHQ-9 missiles are also believed to be effective at altitudes of up to 75,000 feet.[59]

China has further modified the HHQ-9 for use on board the Luyang III (Type 052D), China's latest guided missile destroyer, first commissioned in March 2014. This new destroyer hosts the HHQ-9B air defense system, which is an upgraded version of the HHQ-9, so its lineage can also be traced directly back to the Russian S-300. The HHQ-9B surface-to-air missile used in the Luyang III, extends the range of its predecessor out to a distance of 120 km against aircraft.[60]

Finally, China's latest frigate, the Jiangkai II–class (Type 054A), is equipped with the new HHQ-16 air defense system. The HHQ-16 is the naval variant of the HQ-16, which is believed to be based on either the Russian SA-11 Gadfly or the SA-17 Grizzly missile system.[61] The HQ-16 also seems to have been the product of a joint Russian-Chinese development project.[62] The U.S. Department of Defense has noted that "[a]ccording to Chinese open press reports, the HQ-16 SAM is a Russian-Chinese codevelopment project, possibly involving SA-11 technology."[63] At any rate, reliance on Russian air defense technology is noteworthy because the Jiangkai II is designed especially to provide medium-range air defense coverage for China's fleet. Thus far, there is little actual performance data available about the HHQ-16, although U.S. intelligence estimates of its range vary between 35 and 75 km.[64]

55. For details on the S-300PMU, see generally Carlo Kopp, "Almaz-Antey S-300PMU2 Favorit Self-Propelled Air Defence System / SA-20 Gargoyle," *Air Power Australia*, Technical Report APA-TR-2009-0502, http://www .ausairpower.net/APA-S-300PMU2-Favorit.html.

56. Kopp, "CPMIEC HQ-9." Note, however, that some sources believe that the HQ-9 missile is not directly based on the 48N6. See "HHQ-9/HHQ-9A," *Jane's Naval Weapon Systems*, January 2, 2015.

57. Richard D. Fisher and Carlo Kopp, "China and Russia Upgrade Anti-Air Systems," *Defense Technology International*, December 1, 2009.

58. ONI, *People's Liberation Army Navy*, 18.

59. "HQ-9/-15 and HHQ-9 (RF-9/-15, FD-2000 and FT-2000)," *Jane's Strategic Weapon Systems*, August 19, 2013.

60. "The Luyang III (Type 052D) Class DDGHM," *Jane's Fighting Ships: 2014–2015*, 140; "HQ-9/-15," *Jane's Strategic Weapon Systems*; ONI, *People's Liberation Army Navy*, 18.

61. Carlo Kopp, "PLA Area Defence Missile Systems," *Air Power Australia*, Technical Report APA-TR-2009-0302, updated April 2012, http://www.ausairpower.net/APA-PLA-IADS-SAMs.html; "China's New Air Defence System Relies on Russian-made Elements," Voice of Russia, September, 16, 2013, http://sputniknews .com/voiceofrussia/2013_09_16/China-s-new-air-defence-system-relies-on-Russian-made-elements-6754/; "Hongqi-16 (HQ-16)," missilethreat.com, http://missilethreat.com/defense-systems/hongqi-16-hq-16/#fn-16093-1; "SA-17 GRIZZLY / Buk-M2 SA-N-12 GRIZZLY / *Yezh* HQ-16," globalsecurity.org, http://www.globalsecurity.org /military/world/russia/sa-17.htm.

62. "CF-2000," *Jane's Strategic Weapon Systems*, March 6, 2014; Kopp, "PLA Area Defence"; *DOD China Report 2000*, 18.

63. *DOD China Report 2000*, 18.

64. ONI, *People's Liberation Army Navy*, 18. For more information on the HHQ-16, see also http://www .armyrecognition.com/china_chinese_army_missile_systems_vehicles/hq-16a_ly-80_ground_to_air_defence _missile_system_technical_data_sheet_specifications_pictures_video.html; "Hongqi-16," missilethreat.com.

Air Defense Systems Acquired Outright from Russia or Derived from Russian Technology

Class	Manufacturer	Type	Range	Deployed Ships
SA-N-7 Gadfly	Russia	Air defense	25 km	Sovremenny
SA-N-12 Shtil (Grizzly)	Russia	Air defense	35 km	Luyang I
SA-N-20 Fort	Russia	Air defense	150 km	Luzhou
HHQ-9	China	Air defense	100–120 km	Luyang II–III
HHQ-16	China	Air defense	Est. 35–75 km	Jiangkai II
Band Stand (Mineral ME)	Russia	Surface surveillance and tracking	250–450 km	Sovremenny, Luzhou, Luyang I–III, Jiangkai II
Top Plate (Fregat MAE-3)	Russia	Air surveillance	180 km	Sovremenny, Luzhou, Luyang I
Front Dome (Orekh)	Russia	Fire control	Unknown	Sovremenny, Luyang I, Jiangkai II
Tomb Stone	Russia	Fire control	200–300 km	Luzhou

Sources: See *Jane's Fighting Ships: 2014–2015*, 136–140; ONI, *People's Liberation Army Navy*, 18; *Rosoboronexport Catalog*, 82–3; Diakadis, *China's Defense Strategy*, 193; Mineral ME IHS Janes, February 2, 2015.

Impact of Russian Air Defense Support

As recently as 2000, a U.S. Department of Defense study on China's military noted:

> Currently, the PLAN's surface units are ill equipped for air defense, particularly [against] ASCMs. Only a handful of the PLAN's approximately 60 destroyers and frigates are equipped with SAMs [surface-to-air missiles]; the remainder are outfitted with anti-aircraft guns of various calibers. The few existing SAM systems have extremely limited ranges and are useful only for point defense. No long-range ship-borne SAM systems currently exist in the inventory.[65]

Today, the story is very different. Since 2000, China's fleet modernization program has emphasized improvement of its air defense capabilities. Currently, Chinese warships host an assortment of Russian air defense systems as well as Chinese-built systems derived from Russian technology. These systems are providing significantly improved air defense capability for China's surface fleet. In its 2009 report, the U.S. Office of Naval Intelligence acknowledged these improvements, noting that "[i]n recent years, the most notable upgrade to the PLA(N) surface force has been its shipboard area-air-defense (AAD) capability."[66]

Russian technology has been especially important for those Chinese ships designed specifically for air defense. For example, China's Sovremenny destroyers were purchased in part for their air defense capabilities. As previously noted, the SA-N-7 Gadfly hosted on the Sovremennys extended the range of Chinese air defense systems from just 13 km for

---

65. *DOD China Report 2000*, 18.
66. ONI, *People's Liberation Army Navy*, 18. See also ONI, *People's Liberation Army Navy*, 15.

the legacy HQ-7 Crotale out to 25 km. This upgrade gave the PLAN its first medium-range air defense capability. With the addition of the Russian SA-N-12 Shtil on the new Luyang I destroyers, China's air defense coverage was extended out to a range of 35 km.

China acquired its first long-range air defense capability with deployment of the Russian SA-N-20 on Chinese Luzhou-class destroyers. The SA-N-20 effectively extended China's naval air defense umbrella out to a distance of 150 km. China's Luyang II–class destroyers, meanwhile, outfitted with the domestically produced though Russian-derived HHQ-9, provide long-range air defense capability out to a range of 100 km (120 km for the HHQ-9B).

Most recently, the HHQ-16 air defense system, installed on the new Jiangkai II–class frigates and derived in part from Russian technology, offers a powerful new medium-range air defense capability for the PLAN. Although its range is considerably less than that provided by either the SA-N-20 or the HHQ-9, the HHQ-16, when used in combination with the Jiangkai's vertical launch system and its powerful Chinese phased-array radar system (the Aegis-like Type 382 air defense radar), makes the Jiangkai II the most effective medium-range air defense platform in the Chinese navy.

It should also be noted that Russian air defense radar systems, at the time they were first transferred, represented a marked improvement over China's existing radar systems. For example, the Top Plate surveillance radar system deployed on the Sovremenny-, Luzhou-, and Luyang I–class destroyers represented a notable upgrade to the Chinese Type 381 Rice Shield radar systems installed on the older Luhai-class destroyer. The Rice Shield was at the time a reasonably advanced radar system when compared with other PLAN radars. The most modern variant of the Top Plate family can detect targets out to 230 km (vs. 180 km for the Type 381), while the latter also suffers from inaccuracy and limited beam-steering capabilities.[67] Russian fire control radar systems, such as the Tomb Stone, also represented significant improvements for the fleet.

Recently, however, China appears to have closed the gap with Russia in certain categories of advanced radar technology. New radar systems, such as the Type 346 Dragon Eye installed on the Luyang I– and II–class destroyers, and the Type 382 phased-array radar system installed on the Jiangkai II frigate, are quite advanced in comparison with Russian radar systems. They have even been compared favorably with U.S. Aegis-style phased-array radars, which represent the world standard. The emergence of these new systems demonstrates China's growing independence from Russia in the production of advanced air surveillance radar systems. Despite such progress, Russian air defense radar systems are likely to contribute to the PLAN's air defense mission in other areas for some time to come.

---

67. Richard D. Fisher, Jr., *The Impact of Foreign Weapons and Technology on the Modernization of China's People's Liberation Army* (report for the U.S.-China Economic and Security Review Commission, January 2004), 48, http://bugler-john.50megs.com/MIL.TECH.%20TRANS.%20TO%20PRC.PDF.

4 | Impact of Russian Military Transfers on China's Surface Warfare Capabilities

Having now surveyed Russia's overall contribution to China's surface warfare capabilities in terms of ships, sensors, weapons, and technology, this section will evaluate how those specific systems are actually contributing to China's growing anti-access capabilities.

Enhanced Anti-Ship Strike Capabilities

Russian ASCMs, radar systems, and related technology have significantly enhanced China's ability to conduct precision strikes against U.S. surface warships. The ability to place American warships at risk from long range lies at the very heart of China's anti-access strategy. Since the end of the Cold War, the U.S. Navy has been able to operate virtually uncontested in the world's oceans, allowing it to safely project power overseas as and when it deems appropriate. Having the ability to put U.S. warships at risk in the open oceans directly attacks the preferred U.S. strategy of operating safely from ocean sanctuaries. The provision of advanced Russian sensors and anti-ship missiles has therefore helped China to overcome the first of the three shortcomings mentioned above, the large disparity in anti-ship striking power that formerly existed between U.S. and Chinese maritime forces.

SURFACE SEARCH AND TRACKING SYSTEMS

Advanced Russian ship-borne radar systems have significantly improved China's ability to detect, track, and target U.S. warships at sea. Even with today's advanced technologies, finding and tracking moving ships at sea remain formidable challenges. Yet the ability to detect and track ships at a distance before they gain access to contested maritime regions is an absolute requirement for China's anti-access strategy to succeed. Without this ability, China's large inventory of anti-ship missiles would be of little use. Until recently, however, China's ship-based ISR systems were quite limited, forcing the fleet to depend primarily on maritime aircraft and long-range shore-based sensors.

Advanced Russian systems, such as the Top Plate, have been instrumental for improving China's long-range ISR capabilities. Although Top Plate is designed primarily for aerial surveillance (as discussed above), it can also detect surface targets out to the ship's line-of-sight range.[1] Top Plate also offers the ability to perform "effectively in intensive ECM [electronic countermeasure] environment[s],"[2] giving the PLAN enhanced surface surveillance capability when facing electronic attack.

The Sovremenny's Palm Frond radar system also provides significant surface search capabilities. Although the Palm Frond is often described as a navigation radar, it also provides extended surveillance capability for detecting and locating surface warships.[3] Although open source data on the Palm Frond is limited, Rosoboronexport, Russia's state-owned arms export company, indicates that the Palm Frond is capable of determining target locations and displaying them on tactical situation maps.[4]

Russia's most important ship-borne ISR contribution has been the Mineral-E Band Stand radar system, which provides advanced surface search and tracking for a range of Russian- and Chinese-made ASCMs. In 2009, the U.S. Office of Naval Intelligence cited the Band Stand radar as one of the key reasons for China's improved OTH targeting capabilities.[5] The Band Stand radar is currently installed on Sovremenny-, Luzhou-, and Luyang-class destroyers as well as Jiangkai II–class frigates. The extent to which Chinese warships still rely on the Band Stand is testament to its superior capabilities.

ASCM SYSTEMS

China's ability to target U.S. warships in the open oceans has been vastly improved by deployment of a range of sophisticated Russian ASCMs and, more recently, Chinese ASCMs built using Russian technology. Despite these new systems, successfully attacking U.S. warships at sea remains a difficult challenge. A successful strike typically requires advanced OTH targeting capability, automated command and control systems, and sophisticated ASCMs. U.S. warships employ a range of countermeasures to thwart such attacks, including mobility, electronic countermeasures, and layered defensive systems designed to intercept incoming cruise missiles in flight.

Moreover, the PLAN must also be able to strike U.S. surface warships quickly and at the longest possible range once they are detected. In force-on-force engagements between surface fleets, the ability to strike first is paramount.[6] Analysis of past naval battles demonstrates that in an engagement between comparable surface forces, the side that strikes effectively first generally prevails, because the initial salvo will reduce the size of the enemy force, leaving the attacking force with an enduring advantage in terms of total numbers and aggregate firepower. The force that strikes first can then exploit this advantage by sustaining and concentrating its superior firepower against the now-diminished

1. *Rosoboronexport Catalog*, 82–3, http://www.scribd.com/doc/30810999/Rosoboronexport-Naval-Systems -Catalogue#scribd.
2. Ibid.
3. Ibid., 88–9.
4. Ibid.
5. ONI, *People's Liberation Army Navy*, 18.
6. See generally Wayne P. Hughes, *Fleet Tactics and Coastal Combat* (Annapolis, MD: Naval Institute Press, 2000), 40–44, 266–309.

Comparison of Select Chinese and U.S. ASCMs

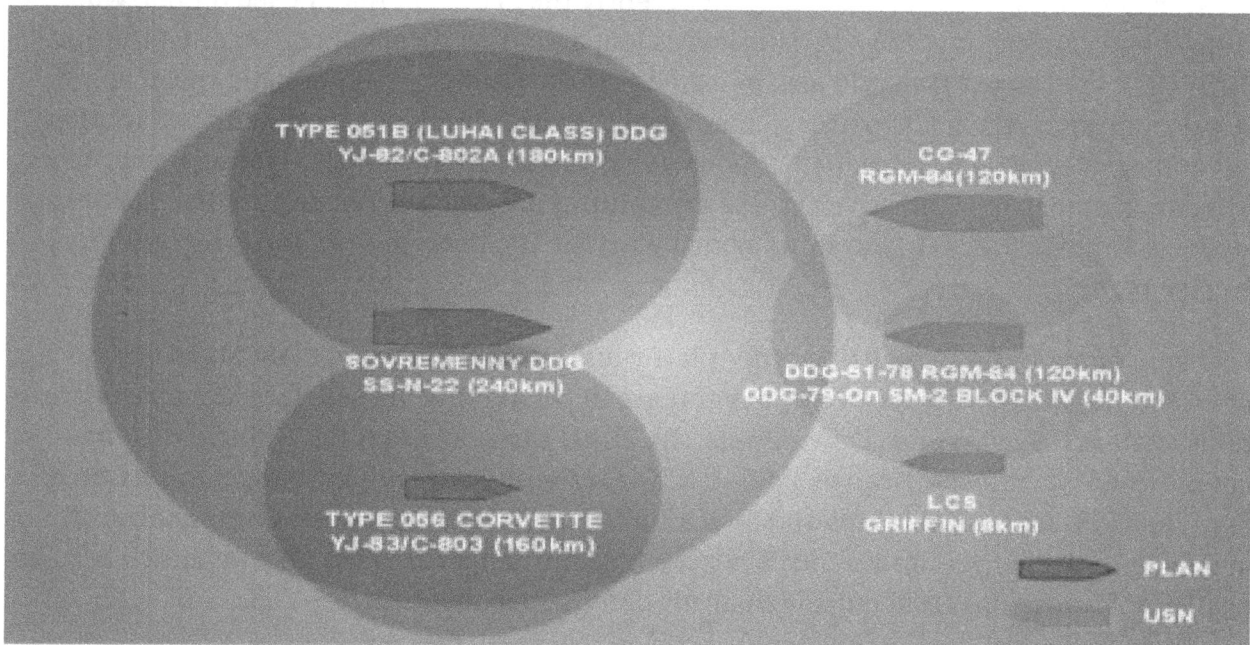

TYPE 051B (LUHAI CLASS) DDG
YJ-82/C-802A (180km)

CG-47
RGM-84(120km)

SOVREMENNY DDG
SS-N-22 (240km)

DDG-51-78 RGM-84 (120km)
DDG-79-On SM-2 BLOCK IV (40km)

TYPE 056 CORVETTE
YJ-83/C-803 (160km)

LCS
GRIFFIN (8km)

PLAN

USN

Source: Reprinted with permission of Delex Systems Inc. from Timothy A. Walton and Bryan McGrath, "China's Surface Fleet Trajectory: Implications for the U.S. Navy," chapter 8 in *China's Near Seas Combat Capabilities*, China Maritime Study No. 11, ed. Peter Dutton, Andrew S. Erickson, and Ryan Martinson (Newport, RI: Naval War College, February 2014), 123.

fleet of the adversary until it either withdraws or is destroyed.[7] Of course, in a force-on-force engagement, having the ability to outrange the opponent gives a fleet the means to strike before the enemy can close to within striking range of its own weapons, particularly if the attacking fleet's own weapons have the penetrating capability to overcome the adversary's ship-based self-defense systems.

In other kinds of engagements, such as that between a submarine and a surface warship, the ability to strike first can be obtained by means other than outranging the opponent, although range still matters. By operating underwater, a submarine can stealthily approach the target and use the element of surprise to launch a devastating first strike. Likewise, aircraft, because of their high speed, long range, and great mobility, are capable of approaching rapidly to within range of enemy warships to initiate a first strike.

Russian ASCMs have given China significantly improved striking power against U.S. warships, both symmetrically in force-on-force engagements and asymmetrically in engagements in which other platforms are used, such as aircraft and submarines. In force-on-force engagements, long-range Russian ASCMs have given the PLAN a distinct first-strike advantage against U.S. surface warships. For example, the Sunburn missile provided with the Russian Sovremenny destroyer has given China a substantial range advantage over

---

7. Ibid., 266–309.

its U.S. counterpart. According to a recent article published by the U.S. Naval War College, the Harpoon missile (RGM-84), which is currently the principal ASCM used on U.S. warships, has a range of just 120 km. This leaves it at a distinct disadvantage against the Sunburn's 240 km range.[8] It should also be noted that the Sunburn's supersonic speed at sea-skimming levels and superior maneuverability provide the Chinese with yet another advantage over the U.S. subsonic Harpoon, which lacks the better penetrating power of its Russian counterpart. Collectively, these capabilities give the Sovremenny a distinct first-strike advantage over U.S. warships armed with the Harpoon in a potential force-on-force engagement.

For asymmetric attacks using other platforms, Russian long-range ASCMs have also provided the PLAN with important advantages in conducting anti-surface warfare operations against U.S. warships. For example, the PLAN can now use quiet Kilo-class submarines armed with the long-range 3M-54E Klub Sizzler missile (220 km range) to stealthily approach U.S. surface warships and attack them from range. Likewise, Chinese aircraft armed with the long-range Kh-59MK missile (285 km range) are now able to launch attacks against U.S. warships from outside their air defense perimeters.

The use of long-range ASCMs complicates the task of the defender in two ways. First, because of the greater range of their ASCMs, Chinese aircraft and submarines no longer have to approach U.S. warships quite as closely in order to conduct an effective strike. Having this standoff capability makes them less vulnerable to counterstrikes by U.S. aircraft, shipborne surface-to-air missiles, and ASW systems. Moreover, because Chinese aircraft and submarines can now strike from greater distance, U.S. surveillance systems and combat air patrols must now cover a much larger area in order to detect their approach. This greatly complicates the task of surveillance, and requires the United States to commit additional resources to the task.

While it is true that China now produces indigenous ASCMs with ranges comparable or even superior to those of the Russian ASCMs (e.g., the YJ-62 ASCM has a range of 280 km[9]), Chinese ASCMs lack many of the advanced features of their Russian counterparts, including supersonic speed, exceptional maneuverability, and superior penetrating power. Thus, China's Russian-built ASCMs still remain better suited for the anti-surface warfare mission, especially against sophisticated U.S. defensive systems. With the development of new Chinese missiles, like the YJ-12 and YJ-18, the situation is starting to change. Such missiles have characteristics, including long range and supersonic speed, comparable to those of their Russian counterparts. This should not be surprising, since, as noted above, many analysts have concluded that such missiles were derived from Russian missiles, such as the 3M-54E Klub Sizzler and the Kh-31 Krypton.[10] So even in this case, Russia's contribution has been critical.

---

8. Walton and McGrath, "China's Surface Fleet," 123.
9. Gormley et al., *Force Multiplier*, 34. (400 km according to some sources. Gormley et al., "Potent Vector," 101.)
10. Gormley et al., "Potent Vector," 102.

Of course, the United States does not rely solely on ship-based anti-ship weapons to defend its fleet against Chinese warships in a force-on-force engagement. Consequently, the range advantage that China enjoys should not be seen as the sole criterion for comparing the capabilities of the respective fleets. U.S. submarines, stealth aircraft, and other systems are intended to play a key role in conducting strikes against PLAN warships. Nor is the United States lacking in countermeasures to protect the fleet against asymmetric ASCM attacks from other Chinese platforms. The United States maintains systems capable of attacking those platforms directly, before they can launch their missiles, and the United States also deploys sophisticated systems to intercept incoming cruise missiles while in flight.[11]

Nevertheless, the fact that Chinese warships have now obtained certain anti-surface warfare advantages over their U.S. counterparts is already forcing changes in the U.S. force posture. The U.S. Navy, for example, recently launched a program to develop a new long-range ASCM aptly referred to as the Long-Range Anti-Ship Missile (LRASM). The rationale for the LRASM is to help in "maintaining the survivability and mission effectiveness of Navy surface combatants when operating within range of Chinese surface combatants armed with capable ASCMs."[12] The Navy is also actively upgrading its cruise missile defense capabilities by introducing new systems, such as the SM-6 active-radar missile, which is improving its capability for intercepting incoming cruise missiles.

Enhanced Air Defense Capabilities

Russian air defense systems and technology have enhanced China's ability to provide the kind of fleet-based air defense umbrella needed for the PLAN to give full effect to its anti-access strategy. In order to deny access to U.S. carrier task forces operating in the western Pacific, the PLAN's surface fleet will need to be able to defend against U.S. air attack. Only in this way can China's warships stay in the battle long enough to bring their enhanced striking power to bear against U.S. warships attempting to gain access to contested theaters in the western Pacific. Having the ability to put U.S. aircraft at greater risk in conducting air strikes against China's fleet eliminates one of the key advantages enjoyed by the U.S. military in recent years, namely, the ability to conduct unimpeded air and missile strikes against enemy warships. This U.S. advantage has been so overwhelming that no recent adversary has even dared to attempt a confrontation. By eroding this advantage, Russia's contribution to naval air defense has helped China to overcome the second of the three shortcomings mentioned above, its limited maritime air defense capability against U.S. aerial attack.

---

11. U.S. cruise missile defense systems, based on ship-borne SM-6 missiles, E-2D airborne radar systems, and combat interceptors armed with AIM-120 missiles, are capable of intercepting incoming cruise missiles, subject to range limitations of the SM-6 and the E-2D radar systems, as well as the availability of sufficient combat interceptors to provide adequate perimeter defense.

12. Ronald O'Rourke, *China's Naval Modernization: Implications for U.S. Navy Capabilities—Background and Issues for Congress* (Washington, DC: U.S. Congressional Research Service, 2014), 57, http://fas.org/sgp/crs/row/RL33153.pdf.

Comparison of Select Chinese and U.S. Naval Air Defense

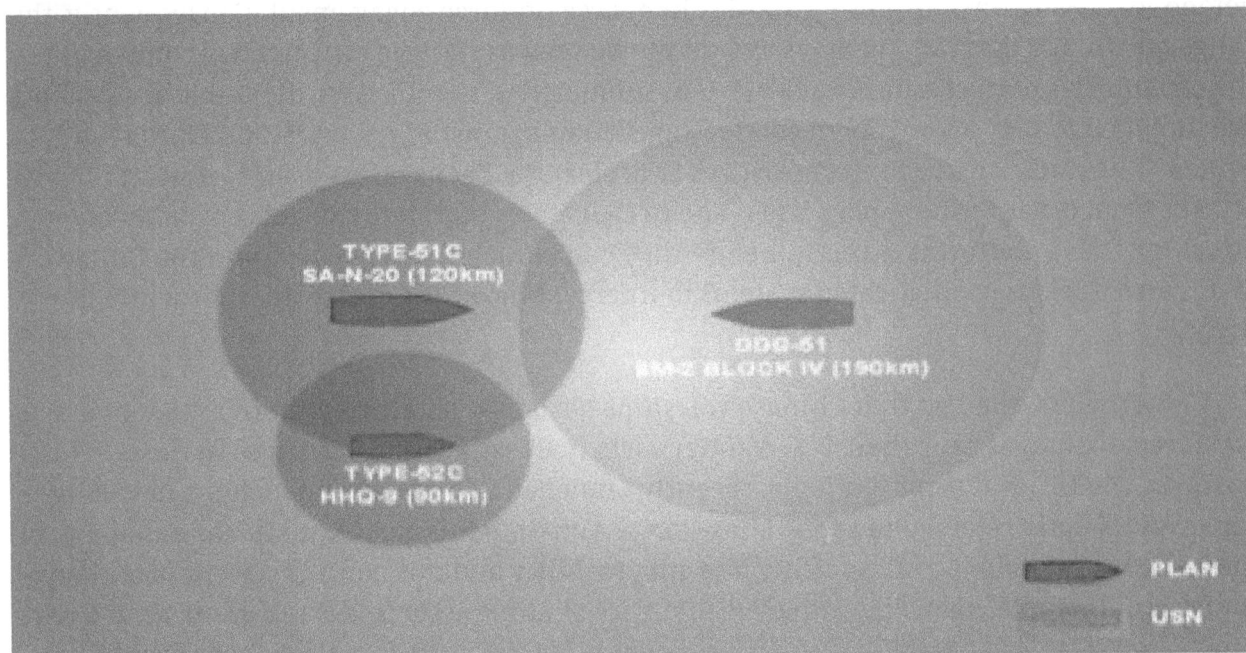

TYPE-51C
SA-N-20 (120km)

DDG-51
SM-2 BLOCK IV (150km)

TYPE-52C
HHQ-9 (90km)

PLAN
USN

Source: Reprinted with permission of Delex Systems Inc. from Timothy A. Walton and Bryan McGrath, "China's Surface Fleet Trajectory: Implications for the U.S. Navy," chapter 8 in *China's Near Seas Combat Capabilities,* China Maritime Study No. 11, ed. Peter Dutton, Andrew S. Erickson, and Ryan Martinson (Newport, RI: Naval War College, February 2014), 121.

AIR SURVEILLANCE SYSTEMS

Improving the fleet's ability to detect, track, and target enemy aircraft and inbound anti-ship missiles at greater range has been a key requirement for China's anti-access strategy. After all, without effective long-range ISR systems, China's newly acquired long-range surface-to-air missile systems would have a much greater challenge in defending fleet warships against incoming aircraft and missiles, because their crews would be unable to locate them at tactically meaningful distances. Russian ship-borne radar systems have been instrumental in upgrading the PLAN's ISR capabilities against enemy air and missile strikes. In fact, the U.S. Office of Naval Intelligence recently cited China's use of "advanced air-surveillance systems, including the Russian Tombstone [*sic*] and Top Plate," as key factors enabling China to upgrade its "shipboard area-air-defense (AAD) capability."[13] With Top Plate providing enhanced long-range aerial surveillance, and Tomb Stone providing extended range tracking and engagement of multiple targets and advanced missile guidance functionality, these systems represented substantial improvements over China's existing systems.

SURFACE-TO-AIR MISSILE SYSTEMS

Of course, detecting and tracking airborne targets at longer range is only half the battle. The PLAN must also be able to effectively engage such targets at range. Long-range

---

13. ONI, *People's Liberation Army Navy,* 18.

engagement is necessary for two reasons. First, the capacity to strike enemy aircraft at longer range impedes their ability to conduct standoff missile strikes against PLAN surface warships. The risk of attack forces enemy pilots to make a difficult choice, either to enter the engagement zone of PLAN air defense systems and risk destruction or launch an attack from even greater range, thereby reducing its effectiveness. In the latter case, firing from longer range also gives the PLAN more opportunities to intercept incoming cruise missiles before they can strike.

As noted, Russian air defense systems and technology have helped China to progressively increase the range of its fleet air defense systems. These gains have given China's surface fleet the increased capacity to operate independently in the open oceans, which in turn has given them a better chance to play their expected role in China's anti-access strategy.

Despite such gains, China's air defense capability continues to lag behind that of the United States. According to the same Naval War College Study cited above, the U.S. Aegis combat system, which is deployed with advanced missiles such as the SM-2, enjoys a significant range advantage over its Chinese counterparts.[14] This advantage will be important in a fleet encounter between surface warships. For one, the shorter range of Chinese air defense systems enables U.S. aircraft to approach more closely to PLAN warships, enhancing their ability to launch effective strikes against those ships. Correspondingly, the longer range of the U.S. ship-borne air defense systems forces Chinese aircraft to operate at much greater distance from U.S. warships, substantially impeding the Chinese aircraft's effectiveness.

Notwithstanding these retained advantages, the U.S. Navy is currently exploring new methods to maintain its lead over China's evolving naval air defense systems. For example, in a recent article, Al Shaffer, the acting U.S. assistant secretary of defense for research and acquisition, emphasized the need for the United States to acquire both faster, hypersonic missiles and better electronic defense capabilities to counter advanced Russian and Chinese air defense systems, noting that the United States is making progress in developing and testing these weapons.[15]

---

14. Walton and McGrath, "China's Surface Fleet," 121.

15. Kris Osborne, "Pentagon: Hypersonic Missiles Needed to Defeat Russian Air Defense Systems," *DefenseTech*, March 21, 2014, http://defensetech.org/2014/03/21/pentagon-hypersonic-needed-to-defeat-russian-air-defense-systems/.

5 | Conclusion and Likely Future Direction of Russian Support

Russian arms and technology transfers have had a major impact on the development of China's surface and anti-surface warfare capabilities. Since the Cold War, Russia has provided China with a steady stream of sophisticated armaments, including surface warships, cruise missiles, air defense systems, and radar systems. The result has been a vast improvement in the air defense and precision strike capabilities of China's maritime forces. Moreover, Russian technology transfers have given China's defense industry a significant boost in developing and producing sophisticated new surface and anti-surface warfare systems, although in some cases the transfer was achieved through illicit reverse engineering activities.

Nor is this simply a relic of history. Recently, for example, Russia and China reportedly have reached agreement on the transfer of the cutting-edge S-400 air defense system. The Russians are also reportedly developing a naval version of the S-400, though its deployment seems to have been delayed.[1] Nevertheless, if the naval variant is both developed and transferred to the Chinese, it would further double the effective range of China's naval air defense capabilities. Moreover, new Russian-derived Chinese missiles such as the YJ-12 and YJ-18 represent a significant leap forward in Chinese cruise missile production capabilities, and indicate that China is still absorbing and benefiting from previous Russian arms and technology transfers, and is likely to continue to do so.

While Russian military systems and related technology have clearly played a crucial role in the development of China's naval air defense and anti-surface warfare capabilities, the level of Russian transfers has declined in recent years. China's increased ability to develop and produce the necessary systems internally has been a key factor. China's shipyards are now quite capable of constructing modern navy ships, with advanced hull designs and indigenously produced power plants. China also now produces most of the onboard systems domestically.

The decline in Russian arms sales to China after 2006, however, was attributable in part to other reasons. As its defense industry improved, China became less willing to purchase anything but the most advanced Russian systems. Moreover, as a condition for

---

1. Keir Giles, *Russian Ballistic Missile Defense: Rhetoric and Reality* (Carlisle, PA: United States Army War College Press, 2015), 26.

purchasing new Russian systems, China increasingly demanded that Russia agree to transfer the underlying technology as well. As China's military power improved, however, Russia became increasingly reluctant to transfer its most advanced weapon systems and technology, fearing not unreasonably that someday such weapons might be turned against Russia itself. Moscow also was increasingly frustrated by China's reverse engineering practices, which Russia deemed abusive, as copies of previously transferred Russian systems continued to surface. Insult was added to injury when China began to sell some of those systems on the arms export markets, thereby undercutting Russian exports of the original system.

Nevertheless, China continues to utilize Russian equipment and technology in many of the most crucial areas, and Russia continues to sell such systems to China. Advanced Russian cruise missiles, air defense systems, and intelligence, surveillance, and reconnaissance platforms are all contributing in important ways to the PLAN's improved performance and growing anti-access capabilities.

Still, China has made enormous strides in closing the technology gap between itself and Russia. Beijing is increasingly able to manufacture advanced ISR systems and precision strike weapons on its own. For example, the new Aegis-like phased-array radar systems installed on the Luyang II and III destroyers and the Jiangkai II frigates are equal to or better than anything the Russians currently produce. Moreover, most of China's warships are currently equipped with domestically produced ASCMs, like the YJ-62 and YJ-83, rather than Russian models. Both the phased-array radar systems and the YJ-62 and YJ-83 missiles were apparently developed without use of Russian technology.

Additionally, while China may have relied to a greater extent on Russian systems in the past for enhancing its anti-ship missile and air defense capabilities, having now acquired the capacity to produce them domestically, China is less likely to turn to Russia for future assistance in those areas. For example, while China's HHQ-9 and HHQ-16 air defense systems were reportedly developed with Russian assistance and technology, China can likely use the knowledge gained through those programs to develop some new systems on its own in the future. Similarly, although the new YJ-12 and YJ-18 cruise missiles appear to be based on previously provided Russian ASCMs, by reproducing and modifying them itself, China will likely gain the ability to produce similar systems on its own.

Nevertheless, China could continue to benefit from advanced Russian systems and technology in some areas. For example, China still relies to a considerable degree on Russian radar systems, such as the Band Stand, Top Plate, and Tomb Stone, and may continue to purchase these systems from Russia, although some reports indicate that China may have already reverse engineered the Band Stand.[2] Nevertheless, as Russia continues to improve those systems, China may elect to import the improved versions.

---

2. "Is China Making Authorized Knock-Offs of Russian Radars?," *Want China Times,* June 5, 2015, http://www.wantchinatimes.com/news-subclass-cnt.aspx?id=20150605000126&cid=1101.

Moreover, China still seems to lag behind Russia in the production of advanced air defense systems, leading to Beijing's decision to engage Russia to jointly develop the HQ-16, and possibly the HQ-9 as well. China's interest in purchasing the new S-400 air defense platform is another indication that Beijing continues to lag behind Moscow in cutting edge air defense technology.

Furthermore, despite China's demonstrated ability to develop relatively advanced ASCMs, such as the YJ-62, domestically, and notwithstanding the obvious strides Beijing is making to develop new supersonic ASCMs, China could probably still benefit from importing additional Russian ASCM technology. Moscow has unparalleled experience in the development of ASCMs, having been at it now for more than 50 years. Moreover, Russian ASCM programs have not been standing still. Moscow is working on an advanced variant of the Yakhont cruise missile, which reportedly is designed to fly at speeds of up to Mach 4.0 or more.[3] Finally, Russia and China are both trying to develop new hypersonic missiles. Russia appears to be further along in attempts to develop an air-breathing cruise missile (as opposed to a boost glide vehicle) to achieve hypersonic speeds. Conceivably, therefore, China might also turn to Russia for assistance in this area.

Despite the PLAN's recent gains in anti-ship striking capability and air defense, its deficient ASW systems continue to impede its ability to operate offshore, because its surface ships remain vulnerable to attack by advanced U.S. submarines. Russia, by contrast, has had far greater experience in conducting ASW operations against sophisticated U.S. attack submarines, and it manufactures a number of ASW systems, including advanced sonar systems and torpedoes, which could be used to enhance the PLAN's ASW capabilities. Increased Russian involvement in the ASW area is therefore likely as well.

In fact, the current geopolitical situation is ripe for further expansion of the Sino-Russian arms trading relationship. The crisis in Ukraine has left Russia relatively isolated from the West and subject to a broad range of sanctions. To offset these measures, Russia has recently been accelerating its own pivot to Asia. Improving its relations with China has been a central pillar of this strategy. One way to further this goal would be through an increase in Russian military assistance for China. Moreover, the PLA recognizes that it could still benefit from the purchase of advanced Russian military technology, even though it can now satisfy most of its general needs domestically.

China also hopes to take advantage of Russia's diminished bargaining power as a result of the Ukraine crisis to obtain good terms on prospective arms purchases. At this point, however, China is likely to be more selective in what it purchases, buying only the most advanced systems in Russia's inventory. China will also seek technology transfer as a condition of additional purchases. Given Russia's increased geopolitical isolation, Moscow seems more likely to agree to this condition now than it has been for some time. In fact, several large-scale arms transactions that have been in the works for several years are finally

---

3. Presentation by Igor Sutyagin, RUSI, January 1, 2014, https://www.youtube.com/watch?v=UUPKQi4Nbc0.

moving toward completion, in part no doubt because of the changed international landscape created by the Ukraine crisis. These deals include potential sales of the S-400 air defense system, Su-35 combat aircraft, and LADA-class diesel-electric submarines. Prospects for increased arms sales from Russia to China seem greater now than they have been in many years, and not solely in the maritime domain.

About the Author

Paul Schwartz is a nonresident senior associate with the CSIS Russia and Eurasia Program. He is an expert on the Russian military and its defense and security policy, with a special emphasis on Russian defense technology programs, its defense industrial base, Russian arms export programs, and the future development of Russia's military capabilities. He has written extensively on these topics, including several recent articles on the Ukraine crisis, Russia's alleged INF Treaty violations, Sino-Russian defense cooperation, Russia's military modernization programs, and the capabilities of selected Russian weapon systems. He is also a frequent speaker on Russian military and defense policy, and is regularly consulted on such matters by members of the media.

Prior to joining CSIS, Mr. Schwartz had a career of over 20 years working at Hogan & Hartson, an international law firm, and in the defense sector at SAIC and Digital Equipment Corporation. As an attorney with Hogan & Hartson's Technology Law Group, he handled legal matters involving a wide range of emerging technologies for clients worldwide. In the information technology field, he worked on high-level projects for the U.S. military, Department of Defense, and NASA, including the F-22 Program, Air Force Systems Command, U.S. Army Medical R&D Command, and Space Station Freedom Project. Mr. Schwartz holds an M.A. in international relations from the Johns Hopkins School of Advanced International Studies and a J.D. from George Washington University.

www.ingramcontent.com/pod-product-compliance
Lightning Source LLC
Chambersburg PA
CBHW051426290326
41932CB00048B/3240